COLOMBIA

Big Buddy Books

An Imprint of Abdo Publishing
abdopublishing.com

Julie Murray

abdopublishing.com

Published by Abdo Publishing, a division of ABDO, PO Box 398166, Minneapolis, Minnesota 55439.
Copyright © 2016 by Abdo Consulting Group, Inc. International copyrights reserved in all countries. No part of this book may be reproduced in any form without written permission from the publisher. Big Buddy Books™ is a trademark and logo of Abdo Publishing.

Printed in the United States of America, North Mankato, Minnesota.
092015
012016

THIS BOOK CONTAINS
RECYCLED MATERIALS

Cover Photo: Shutterstock.com.
Interior Photos: EITAN ABRAMOVICH/AFP/Getty Images (p. 27); LUIS ACOSTA/AFP/Getty Images (p. 19); RAUL ARBOLEDA/AFP/Getty Images (p. 29); ASSOCIATED PRESS (pp. 9, 15, 31); © Bettmann/CORBIS (p. 11); De Agostini Picture Library/Getty Images (p. 16); Eric SA House - Carle/ Getty Images (p. 5); JEFF HAYNES/AFP/Getty Images (p. 33); © iStockphoto.com (p. 38); Kaveh Kazemi/Getty Images (pp. 11, 34); © Herbert Kehrer/Corbis/Glow Images (p. 23); Bryn Lennon/Getty Images (p. 17); Sandro Pereyra/STR/Getty Images (p. 34); LUIS ROBAYO/AFP/Getty Images (p. 17); Shutterstock.com (pp. 5, 9, 13, 19, 21, 23, 25, 27, 31, 35, 37, 38).

Coordinating Series Editor: Megan M. Gunderson
Editor: Katie Lajiness
Contributing Editor: Marcia Zappa
Graphic Design: Adam Craven

Country population and area figures taken from the CIA World Factbook.

Library of Congress Cataloging-in-Publication Data

Murray, Julie, 1969-
  Colombia / Julie Murray.
     pages cm. -- (Explore the countries (Set 3))
  Includes index.
  ISBN 978-1-68078-066-6
1. Colombia--Juvenile literature. I. Title.
  F2258.5.M88 2016
  986.1--dc23
                           2015023794

COLOMBIA

CONTENTS

Around the World 4

Passport to Colombia 6

Important Cities 8

Colombia in History 12

Timeline 16

An Important Symbol 18

Across the Land 20

Earning a Living 24

Life in Colombia 26

Famous Faces 30

Tour Book 34

A Great Country 36

Colombia Up Close 38

Important Words 39

Websites 39

Index 40

AROUND THE WORLD

Our world has many countries. Each country has beautiful land. It has its own rich history. And, the people have their own languages and ways of life.

Colombia is a country in South America. What do you know about Colombia? Let's learn more about this place and its story!

Did You Know?

Spanish is the official language of Colombia.

SAY IT

Cartagena
kahr-tah-GAY-nah

The city of Cartagena is popular with visitors. It is known for its colorful buildings.

Colombia is the only American nation named for famous explorer Christopher Columbus.

Passport to Colombia

Colombia is in northwestern South America. Venezuela, Brazil, Peru, Ecuador, and Panama border Colombia. The Pacific Ocean and the Caribbean Sea also border Colombia.

Colombia is the fourth-largest country in South America. Its total area is 439,736 square miles (1,138,910 sq km). More than 46 million people live there.

WHERE IN THE WORLD?

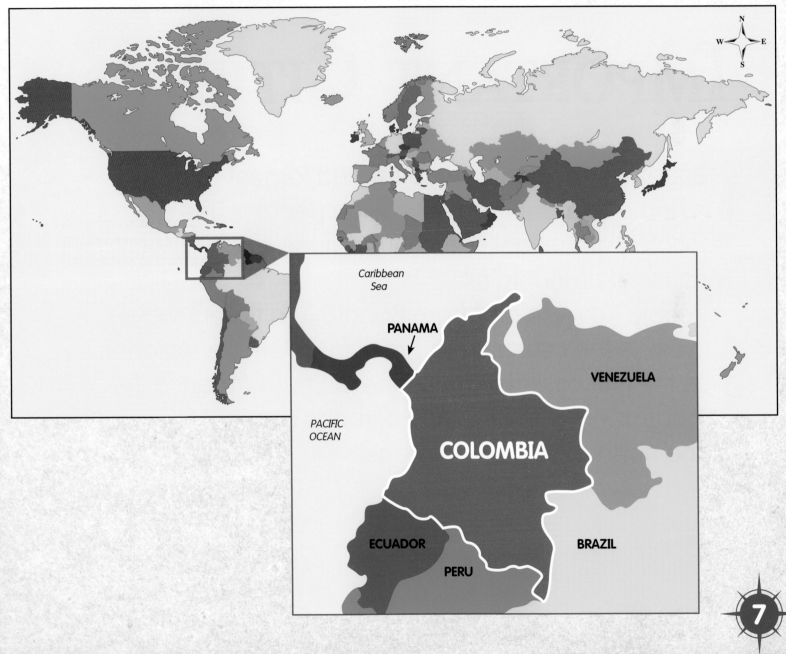

Caribbean Sea

PANAMA

PACIFIC OCEAN

COLOMBIA

VENEZUELA

ECUADOR

PERU

BRAZIL

IMPORTANT CITIES

Bogotá is Colombia's **capital** and largest city. It is home to more than 7.7 million people. This city is located at the foot of the Guadalupe and Monserrate Mountains.

People travel to and from Bogotá in different ways. The city is the center of air travel in Colombia. Avianca was the first **commercial** airline in South America. Its headquarters is in Bogotá. Railroads connect the city to the northern Caribbean coast.

SAY IT

Bogotá
boh-goh-TAH

Bogotá is known for its street art. Artists paint murals on public spaces in the city.

Plaza Bolívar is a historical area of Bogotá. Its cathedral is the largest in Colombia.

Medellín is Colombia's second-largest city, with about 2.4 million people. Medellín began as a mining town in 1675. Now, the city has many clothing factories. And, the area around Medellín grows a lot of the coffee for Colombia.

Cali is Colombia's third-largest city. It has a population of more than 2.3 million people. Cali is the only major Colombian city near the Pacific coast.

SAY IT

Medellín
meh-duh-LEEN

Medellín has many modern buildings. This includes schools and libraries built by the city. The Spain Library is held in three unusual-looking buildings. They look like giant rocks rising from the earth.

Cali hosted the Pan American Games in 1971. It is the only Colombian city ever to host the games. The Pan American Games are similar to the Olympics, but only countries in North and South America participate.

Colombia in History

In 1500, the Spanish first came to Colombia's Caribbean coast. Soon, they started to bring goods back including gold and chocolate.

During the mid-1600s, Spain built Castillo de San Felipe de Barajas. It was the largest castle Spain had ever built in the Americas. Spain made the castle to help guard Cartagena and its goods.

In 1717, Spain created a large area called New Granada. Present-day Colombia, Ecuador, Panama, and Venezuela became part of New Granada.

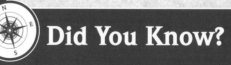

Did You Know?

Pirates sailed the Caribbean coast near Cartagena looking to steal prized goods.

Castillo de San Felipe de Barajas is now a popular place for visitors.

SAY IT

Castillo de San Felipe de Barajas
kas-TEE-yoh day san fay-LEE-pay day bah-RAH-hahs

In 1810, people in Bogotá fought for freedom. Colombia gained independence from Spain. Colombian Independence Day is honored on July 20.

From 1899 to 1903, the Liberal and Conservative political parties fought in the War of a Thousand Days. Up to 130,000 people died in this **civil war**. The war ended with a peace agreement. It promised to make changes within the government and hold fair elections.

In 2014, Colombia played in the soccer World Cup. This was the country's first appearance in the World Cup in 16 years. Colombia lost to Brazil in the quarterfinals.

Independence Day is a national holiday in Colombia. Colombians watch parades while they honor their country.

TIMELINE

1948–1957

Colombian Conservative and Liberal political parties fought for power. This period is known as *La Violencia*. More than 200,000 people died. In 1957, the Liberal and Conservative Parties agreed to share government power. They traded office every other term until 1974.

Before 1500

Before the Spanish came to what is now Colombia, native tribes lived in the area. They were mostly in the western mountains. The different tribes lived close together and worked on farms.

1549

Spain established a colony in Colombia. Then, many native people died. They were not used to the new European sicknesses.

1991

Many changes were made to Colombia's **constitution**. For example, the president must get more than 50 percent of the votes to win an election. If no one receives that many votes, a second election is held.

2010

Colombia's largest soccer stadium opened near Cali. It holds 52,000 people.

2012

Colombia won eight medals in the Summer Olympics. Mariana Pajon won a gold medal for a BMX biking event. In BMX events, riders race around a dirt track with hills.

AN IMPORTANT SYMBOL

The Colombian flag was adopted in 1861. It has three stripes that are yellow, blue, and red. The yellow stripe takes up the top half of the flag.

Colombia's government is a **republic**. The president of Colombia is the chief of state and head of government. He or she is elected for a four-year term.

There are several possible meanings for the colors in Colombia's flag. One idea is yellow stands for gold, blue for seas, and red for blood.

Juan Manuel Santos was elected president in 2014 for a second term.

ACROSS THE LAND

Colombia's land is very **diverse**. It has forests, meadows, and mountains. Because of this, the weather is different across the country. But, the weather in each area stays mostly the same throughout the year.

Colombia has many different plants and trees. An **orchid** is Colombia's national flower. The wax palm is Colombia's national tree. Much of Colombia's rain forests are national forests. People want to save these areas from being torn down.

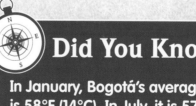

Did You Know?

In January, Bogotá's average temperature is 58°F (14°C). In July, it is 57°F (14°C).

Wax palm trees are the tallest palm trees in the world. They can grow up to 200 feet (60 m) tall!

Many types of animals live in Colombia. Turtles, lizards, snakes, and crocodiles are in Colombia's forests. More than 1,500 different kinds of birds live in the country.

Andean condors are popular birds in Colombia. They have bald heads. The males have white feathers that form collars around their necks. Andean condors often live in the mountains and eat dead animals.

The Andean condor is Colombia's national bird. It is one of the largest flying birds in the world. It can measure 10 feet (3 m) from wing tip to wing tip.

Many interesting animals live in Colombia's rain forests. Cutting down the forests leaves many without a home. This includes the brown spider monkey, which is at risk of disappearing altogether.

EARNING A LIVING

Colombia has one of the fastest-growing **economies** on earth. Many people work to **harvest** food. The country is a major producer of sugar, coffee, corn, and rice.

Transportation is big business in Colombia. Many people work for airlines. Flights connect all of the country's large cities. This helps limit the time it takes to travel through the mountains.

Large numbers of Colombian workers make yarn and cloth. Much of these goods are sent to other countries.

Did You Know?

Colombia is one of the world's largest coal suppliers.

Colombia is famous for growing coffee. Many people in the country work to harvest coffee beans.

LIFE IN COLOMBIA

Colombia has a rich, lively society. People in Colombia enjoy the arts. There are many music halls and places to see paintings. Colombia is also known for its talented writers.

Common Colombian foods include rice with coconut, beans, and pig skin. Many people drink a black coffee called *tinto*.

Soccer is the most popular sport in Colombia. People cheer on the national soccer team. *Tejo* is Colombia's national sport. It involves throwing steel pucks at a target.

Did You Know?

Colombia's school system includes elementary schools, secondary schools, and advanced training courses. The average person receives 14 years of education.

Children grow up playing soccer in Colombia.

Colombia has many fine-art museums.

Much of Colombia has dry weather from December to March. Many people spend time outside to enjoy the weather when it is not raining. Hiking and biking are popular forms of exercise in Colombia.

Most Colombians belong to the **Roman Catholic Church**. The Spanish brought these beliefs to Colombia in the 1500s.

Most Colombians attend Catholic mass on holidays. Palm Sunday (*above*), Easter, and Christmas are important Catholic holidays.

FAMOUS FACES

Many talented people are from Colombia. Shakira is a singer. Her full name is Shakira Isabel Mebarak Ripoll. She was born on February 2, 1977, in Barranquilla.

Shakira began writing songs and singing in talent shows at age 10. She is famous for her 2006 song "Hips Don't Lie."

Shakira cares about giving back to her country. She started a group to help children in Colombia.

SAY IT

Shakira
shah-KEE-rah

Barranquilla
bahr-ahn-KEE-yah

Did You Know?

From 2013 to 2014, Shakira was a judge on the singing talent show *The Voice*. She helped singers prepare to sing on the show.

A 15-foot iron statue of Shakira stands in her hometown of Barranquilla.

In 2011, Shakira became the first Colombian to be honored with a star on Hollywood Boulevard in California.

Colombia is known for its sportsmen. Juan Pablo Montoya is a race car driver from Bogotá. He was born on September 20, 1975. In 2000, Montoya won the Indianapolis 500. He won this famous car race for a second time in 2015.

Montoya works with children in Colombia's poor neighborhoods. He helps build sports centers for them.

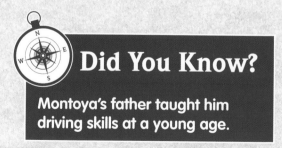

Did You Know?

Montoya's father taught him driving skills at a young age.

Montoya is one of only eight drivers to win the Indianapolis 500 on his first try.

TOUR BOOK

Imagine traveling to Colombia! Here are some places you could go and things you could do.

 **Cheer**

Cheer on Colombia's National Soccer Team. In 2015, this team was ranked fourth in the world!

 **Explore**

The National Coffee Park is in Quindío. Enjoy rides, food, and shows honoring the country's most famous drink.

Eat

Arepas are cakes made of thick cornmeal. Many people add cheese, avocado, meat, and vegetables to their arepas.

Discover

Valle de Cocora is in the center of Colombia's coffee-growing area. It is known for its tall wax palm trees. This area is one of the few places on earth to see these trees.

Travel

Hike into the **jungle** to visit Ciudad Perdida. This city was lost for hundreds of years. The area can only be reached on foot. Visitors come to swim under its waterfalls and explore the old buildings.

A Great Country

The story of Colombia is important to our world. Colombia is a land of beautiful beaches and tall palm trees. It is a country of talented people.

The people and places that make up Colombia offer something special. They help make the world a more beautiful, interesting place.

San Andrés is part of a group of Colombian islands in the Caribbean Sea. Many people visit San Andrés for the pretty water and beaches.

Colombia Up Close

Official Name: Republic of Colombia

Flag:

Population (rank): 46,736,728
(July 2015 est.)
(30th most-populated country)

Total Area (rank): 439,736 square miles
(26th largest country)

Capital: Bogotá

Official Language: Spanish

Currency: Colombian peso

Form of Government: Republic

National Anthem: "Himno Nacional de la Republica de Colombia" (National Anthem of the Republic of Colombia)

IMPORTANT WORDS

capital a city where government leaders meet.

civil war a war between groups in the same country.

commercial (kuh-MUHR-shuhl) meant to make money.

constitution (kahnt-stuh-TOO-shuhn) the basic laws that govern a country or a state.

diverse made up of things that are different from each other.

economy the way that a country produces, sells, and buys goods and services.

harvest to gather ripe crops.

jungle a tropical forest where plants and trees grow very quickly.

orchid a plant with flowers that are brightly colored and that have unusual shapes.

republic a government in which the people choose the leader.

Roman Catholic Church a kind of Christianity that has been around since the first century and is led by the pope.

transportation the act of moving people or things from one place to another.

WEBSITES

To learn more about Explore the Countries, visit **booklinks.abdopublishing.com**. These links are routinely monitored and updated to provide the most current information available.

39

INDEX

animals **22, 23**

Barranquilla **30, 31**

Bogotá **8, 9, 14, 20, 32, 38**

businesses **8, 10, 24, 25, 35**

Cali **10, 11, 17**

Caribbean Sea **6, 8, 12, 37**

Cartagena **5, 12**

Castillo de San Felipe de Barajas **12, 13**

Ciudad Perdida **35**

Columbus, Christopher **5**

food **26, 34, 35**

government **14, 16, 17, 18, 19, 38**

Guadalupe Mountains **8**

language **4, 38**

Medellín **10, 11**

Monserrate Mountains **8**

Montoya, Juan Pablo **32, 33**

National Coffee Park **34**

natural resources **10, 24, 25, 35**

Pacific Ocean **6, 10**

Pajon, Mariana **17**

plants **20, 21, 35, 36**

Plaza Bolívar **9**

population **6, 8, 10, 38**

Quindío **34**

religion **9, 28, 29**

San Andrés **37**

Santos, Juan Manuel **19**

Shakira **30, 31**

size **6, 38**

South America **4, 6, 8, 11**

Spain Library **11**

sports **11, 14, 17, 26, 27, 28, 32, 33, 34**

Valle de Cocora **35**

weather **20, 28**